20TH CENTURY
AMERICAN HISTORY
FOR KIDS

20th★CENTURY AMERICAN HISTORY FOR *Kids*

the MAJOR EVENTS THAT SHAPED the PAST and PRESENT

ANDREA BENTLEY

ROCKRIDGE
PRESS

Interior and Cover Designer: Michael Patti
Art Producer: Tom Hood
Editor: Barbara J. Isenberg
Production Editor: Jenna Dutton

Cover illustration © Jonathan Ball, 2020; Photography from Daniels, John T/Library of Congress, p. 4; Photo 12/Alamy, pp. 7, 73; Hilary Morgan/Alamy, p. 10; Gado Images/Alamy, p. 13; Jack Delano for OWI/Library of Congress, p. 14; New York World-Telegram and the Sun Newspaper Photograph Collection/Library of Congress, p. 16; Library of Congress, pp. 19, 20; mccool/Alamy, pp. 24, 25; American Photo Archive/Alamy, pp. 27, 30, 64, 70; RLFE Pix/Alamy, p. 33; HO Images/Alamy, p. 34; FL Historical 1A/Alamy, p. 36; Pictorial Press Ltd/Alamy, p. 39; Niday Picture Library/Alamy, p. 44; World History Archive/Alamy, pp. 47, 84; dpa picture alliance/Alamy, pp. 50, 99; US Army Photo/Alamy, pp. 53, 67; US Navy Photo/Alamy, p. 54; NASA/Alamy, pp. 56, 76, Back Cover; O'Halloran, Thomas J./Library of Congress, p. 59; colaimages/Alamy, p. 60; DeMarsico, Dick/Library of Congress, p. 65; Palumbo, Fred/Library of Congress, p. 74; Historic Collection, p. 79; PF-(usna)/Alamy, p. 87; Martyn Goddard/Alamy, p. 90; US Air Force Photo/Alamy, p. 93; Bill Bachmann/ Alamy, p. 96; Author Photo courtesy of Brad Moore

ISBN: Print 978-1-64739-790-6 | eBook 978-1-64739-475-2
R0

FOR
AVERY CLAIRE,
ALWAYS
KEEP YOUR LOVE
OF LEARNING.
LOVE YOU . . .
MOST!

CONTENTS

INTRODUCTION

The 20th century in America was one of remarkable change and growth. Some might say that civilization advanced more in those years than it had in any century before it, and the United States led the way. Still a young country—after all, it was only 125 years old—America "grew up" quickly in those years. In the early 19th century, explorers made their way on horseback to the Western frontier. By the end of the 20th century, the country could claim that it had planted a flag not just in the West, but on the Moon.

As we grow up, we get lessons from all kinds of sources. Studying history is one of them. When we do so, we learn about all the events that shaped the way we live today. Studying history is important because it helps us understand why certain things are the way they are and teaches us what our ancestors thought about. It also gives us an opportunity to celebrate their successes and learn from their mistakes. Learning from others is important for individual growth.

Many momentous and exciting things happened in America in the 20th century. Women fought for and won the right to vote, the first computers were developed, and, of course, astronauts landed on the Moon. The century also gave us cartoons, rock and roll, and movies. Unfortunately, not everything was always positive—there were several wars, economic problems and violence at home and abroad. All of the events, good and bad, brought about some sort of change that shaped the country into what it is today. By studying these events and changes, we can become better citizens and begin to make our own positive contributions.

As you read this book, it is my hope you will gain a deeper appreciation of the history of 20th-century America. The events chosen for this book all contributed to shaping our nation and left a piece of history behind for you to learn from. I hope you discover new ideas and keep the pages turning.

AMERICA AT THE TURN OF THE CENTURY

As the 1890s came to a close, more and more Americans were moving from the countryside into cities seeking jobs in factories. People began to earn more money with these jobs and were able to enjoy their free time in new ways. Popular entertainment began to grow, and people went out to talk, dance, and listen to music. Jazz music became popular, and nightclubs became the hangout of choice for many young adults. The rise of organized baseball brought another type of entertainment to Americans. Businesses were booming and more people were able to afford household appliances to make everyday life easier.

Outside its borders, the United States emerged as a world power in 1898 after it defeated Spain in the Spanish-American War. Several years later, President Theodore Roosevelt took a strong stance against the British, who had territories in South America. Roosevelt's foreign policy became known as Big Stick diplomacy, a term he borrowed from a West African proverb: "Speak softly and carry a big stick." Roosevelt and his foreign policy agenda helped move the United States into the role of global leader.

CHAPTER ONE

1901 TO 1920

The beginning of the 1900s saw businesses growing and people's lifestyles changing as they moved into cities. But with that growth, people often experienced a decline in social conditions. Many Americans worked long hours in terrible conditions for very little pay. The gap between the rich and the poor began to widen, and some believed new ideas were needed to help fix the growing gap. This time period became known as the Progressive Era, and many reform efforts were put in place to help those who were struggling.

This time was also one of national patriotism on the world stage. Tensions were brewing among countries in Europe, and some Americans wanted to prove the superiority of the United States. Others, however, wanted to remain neutral and not get involved. This tension played out in a variety of ways during the first two decades of the 20th century.

Throughout it all, change was definitely in the air. The country was growing up and taking on a personality all its own. And its people were looking to the future.

The Wright brothers' first flight

The First Airplane Flight: 1903

Orville and Wilbur Wright, two brothers living in Ohio, were fascinated with aviation. The Wright brothers had been building gliders since 1900, and in 1902, they constructed one a person could fly while holding two ropes to control the wings. Though they wanted to soar through the air, the closest they had gotten by then was flying their glider just 600 feet.

The brothers were not satisfied. They wanted to build and fly an engine-powered aircraft controlled by one pilot. Many people thought they were crazy, but they were determined. Unable to find an engine light enough for flight, the brothers decided the only way to reach their goal was to build an engine themselves. With their custom engine, they also designed and built a **propeller** that had a curved top and a flat bottom.

On December 17, 1903, on the beach of Kitty Hawk, North Carolina, the Wright brothers flew the first successful

MEET SAMUEL PIERPONT LANGLEY

The Wright brothers were not the first to try to fly. Samuel Langley was a scientist who also had a passion for flight. He was awarded a grant from the US government in 1898 to work on an airplane, which he called an "aerodrome," capable of carrying a human. It was completed in 1903 before the Wright brothers completed *Flyer I*. He tried to launch the aircraft twice, but it failed both times.

manned flight in a motorized airplane. Aviation history was made. On the first flight, Orville was the pilot; the airplane flew a total of 120 feet, and it was in the air for 12 seconds. The brothers continued flying their airplane, *Flyer I*, three more times that day. The longest flight was the last one, piloted by Wilbur. The airplane flew 852 feet and stayed in the air for 59 seconds.

The success of the airplane flight did not stop there. The brothers returned home to test and perfect their airplane. After a year of more tests, the Wright brothers had an airplane that could fly 40 miles per hour and stay in the air for 30 minutes, flying a distance of 25 miles. Their love of flight helped set the stage for all future aviation advances.

KITTY HAWK, NORTH CAROLINA

Kitty Hawk is located on the Outer Banks of North Carolina. The Wright brothers chose this location for their tests because of the steady wind that blows in from the Atlantic Ocean. At the time of their tests, Kitty Hawk had a 100-foot-high sand dune that was a perfect place to launch their plane.

The Panama Canal in 1913

Building the Panama Canal: 1904–1914

For years, the only way to get goods from the Atlantic Ocean to the Pacific Ocean was for ships to travel all the way around South America, a 7,000-mile journey. A passage, or canal, through the country of Panama would shorten the trip significantly—it was just 50 miles across. In 1880, France began construction of a canal, but after many years, the project remained unsuccessful and the French abandoned it. The United States decided to finish the project, but there were some obstacles to overcome first.

Panama was then a colony of Colombia. US President Theodore Roosevelt offered to buy the

William Gorgas was a US Army surgeon who had a major impact on the building of the Panama Canal. Prior to working in the Canal Zone, he worked in Havana, the capital of Cuba, where he studied the transmission of yellow fever. When he was sent to Panama, he introduced mosquito control measures that significantly prevented illnesses due to yellow fever and malaria.

rights to the canal from the French, but Colombia also wanted payment, and the deal fell through. In 1903, Roosevelt helped Panama win its independence from Colombia. The next year, the United States purchased a 10-mile-wide strip of land from Panama that extended across the country to begin building a canal. This strip of land became known as the Canal Zone.

Now that the United States had the land, another problem arose: mosquitoes were common in Panama, and they spread diseases such as malaria and yellow fever, which caused people to become ill or even die. For construction workers to stay safe, canal workers were ordered to drain swamps, cut grassy areas, cover water supplies and tents with nets, and use oil and insecticide over standing water. This helped cut down on the number of workers who became sick, and construction of the canal resumed.

The Panama Canal was completed in 1914. The first ship made the voyage through the canal from the Atlantic to the Pacific Ocean in August of that year. The United States now had clear access to world trade, and the US Navy had a way to defend the United States and its interests on both coasts.

DANGEROUS WORKING CONDITIONS

The workers who constructed the Panama Canal endured many dangers on the job. In addition to the threat of yellow fever and malaria, workers' lives were threatened by landslides and other consequences of moving tons of dirt. Of the tens of thousands of workers who helped build the canal, approximately 5,600 Americans died.

The British passenger ship *Lusitania* sinking in 1915

World War I: 1914–1918

The causes of World War I are hotly debated among historians. Nevertheless, when fighting began in Europe in 1914, the United States took a neutral stance at first to try to stay out of the war. It became more difficult to stay completely neutral, however, because the United States had economic ties with the Allied Powers, chiefly the countries of Great Britain and France. In addition to giving huge bank loans to these countries, many factories in America began making weapons and steel for the Allies.

As the war progressed, Germany, a member of the Central Powers, successfully used submarines to

MEET PRESIDENT WOODROW WILSON

Woodrow Wilson was the 28th president of the United States. He served two terms, from 1913 to 1921. When World War I began, he favored **isolationism**, as he did not feel the United States should get involved in world issues. His stance soon changed, though, and in his speech before Congress seeking a declaration of war against Germany he proclaimed, "The world must be made safe for democracy." At the war's end, he presented a peace plan known as the Fourteen Points. His plan called for the creation of the League of Nations—a way for countries to resolve disputes before going to war.

sink British warships. Germany suspected, however, that merchant ships carrying goods were also transporting weapons to the Allies. In 1915, the Germans torpedoed the merchant ship *Lusitania*, and of the 1,200 lives lost, 128 were Americans. The United States demanded that Germany stop sinking non-military ships.

The final straw for the United States came in January 1917 when a German telegram was intercepted. Germany wanted to get Mexico on their side and promised to help Mexico reclaim land in the United

States. This became known as the Zimmerman Telegram. The United States entered the war on the side of the Allied Powers in April 1917.

The addition of the American soldiers helped the Allies, and important battles were won. The Central Powers were low on supplies, ammunition, food, troops, and other resources by the time the United States entered the war. On November 11, 1918, Germany surrendered, ending the war. In June 1919, the Treaty of Versailles was signed, and peace terms were finally set. Germany was forced to take much of the blame for the war, and this would impact the start of World War II not long after.

GERMAN U-BOATS

Germany was the first country to use underwater submarines, called U-boats, in wartime. They had only 38 U-boats at the beginning of World War I, but these submarines proved to be valuable weapons against British warships. When a German U-boat sank the merchant ship *Lusitania*, it meant the Germans were no longer only attacking warships. The United States could no longer avoid going to war. By the end of the World War I, Germany had built 334 U-boats with many more in construction.

Black Americans leaving Mississippi in 1939

The Great Migration: 1916–1970

After the Civil War, Black Americans began to leave the South, with the numbers greatly increasing in the early 1900s. Most headed north, but some moved westward. Their main goal was to escape the poor economic conditions for Black Americans in the South and the racial oppression of the many Jim Crow laws that took away their rights. Jim Crow laws were state and local laws that were enacted after the end of the Civil War legalizing segregation—keeping Black people from voting, getting certain jobs, and having other social and political opportunities. Approximately six million Black

MEET LANGSTON HUGHES

Langston Hughes wrote poetry, stories, novels, and plays. He was also a social activist. Known for his accurate portrayals of Black American life, he wrote how people felt, what they experienced, and the highs and lows of the times. He even wrote about his own personal experiences. Hughes was influential during the Harlem Renaissance and is considered one of its leading voices. His works are still being read today.

Americans relocated over several decades to begin new lives. This movement came to be known as the Great Migration.

Although they still faced discrimination in the North, many Black Americans felt that their lives were safer there and they had more job opportunities. With the move, many began to work jobs new to them. Steel mills and automobile factories employed many of the newcomers.

City populations soon grew rapidly. For example, the Black population in Chicago doubled in size, the population in Cleveland tripled, and the population in Detroit increased sixfold. But the growing numbers of Black people weren't always welcomed. Many white people refused to rent to them, for instance, or when they did, the rents were very high. Tensions rose, leading to many **race riots**.

The resulting racial unrest led to the creation of cities within cities, where Black people congregated in certain areas and white people lived and worked in others. In the 1920s, the Harlem neighborhood of New York City rose as a new, Black cultural center. The Harlem Renaissance was born, and with it came new forms of music, art, and literature. Not only was Black culture being recognized, but Black Americans began to take a prominent place in society.

HARLEM RENAISSANCE

The Harlem Renaissance was a turning point in Black culture. During the 1920s, the Harlem neighborhood of New York City attracted many remarkable thinkers as well as artists, writers, and musicians. Their creations had an enormous impact on how Black people saw themselves and their place in society.

Pouring liquor into the sewer in 1921

Prohibition: 1919–1933

As people continued to address increasing social problems caused by the growth of cities and industry during the Progressive Era, many Americans wanted to restrict the manufacturing, sale, and transportation of alcohol. These people, called "prohibitionists," thought alcohol was having a negative effect on society. They argued that heavy drinking, saloons, and **bootlegging** were widespread, and that organized crime was on the rise. (The term "bootleg" comes from the practice of hiding alcohol in the legs of tall boots.) The prohibitionists wanted to see legislation signed to end the drinking of alcohol once and for all.

MEET AL CAPONE

Al Capone, also called Scarface, became known as the Prohibition era's most infamous gangster. He rose to prominence at the age of 26 and led a crime ring in Chicago from 1925 to 1931. He expanded his territory by gunning down rivals who got in his way. By 1927, his wealth had accumulated to $100 million, and he enjoyed fine cigars and gourmet food. In 1931, he was charged with 22 counts of federal income tax evasion and one count of conspiracy to violate Prohibition laws. In 1932, Capone was found guilty on three of the 23 counts and was sent to prison for tax evasion.

In January 1919, the 18th Amendment to the US Constitution was ratified by Congress. The amendment called for legislation to prohibit the manufacture and sale of alcohol. The resulting legislation was called the National Prohibition Act, but it was better known as the Volstead Act, named after Andrew Volstead, who formulated it. It was not successfully enforced and illegal activity continued.

Bottles of medicinal whiskey were sold at drugstores, and bootleggers began smuggling liquor from foreign countries. It did not take long before bootleggers began bottling their own homemade liquor.

Organized crime also rose. To move liquor from where it was made to where people could drink it, organized gangs began to take over bootlegging operations. Gangs soon controlled the entire bootlegging operation, from distilleries to warehouses to transportation channels, and last, to customers at speakeasies, restaurants, or nightclubs. The gangs worked together to expand their territories. Big boss gangsters such as Johnny Torrio, Big Jim Colosimo, and Al Capone soon became well known.

Many Americans still wanted to drink responsibly, and over time, Prohibition became less of an important issue. Prohibition was finally officially repealed with the 21st Amendment on December 5, 1933.

SPEAKEASY

A "speakeasy" is a hidden bar people went to during the Prohibition era. These bars were often run by gangsters and were located in underground dens or dark saloons. In order to get in, people had to whisper a secret password, which is where the term comes from. Needless to say, since drinking alcohol was still illegal, people who went to a speakeasy had to be very careful.

Suffragists in 1917

MR. PRESIDENT YOU SAY "WE ARE INTERESTED IN THE UNITED STATES POLITICALLY SPEAKING, IN NOTHING BUT HUMAN LIBERTY

R. PRESIDENT WHAT WILL YOU DO FOR WOMAN SUFFRAGE

WE DEMAND AN AMENDMENT

MR. PRESIDENT HOW LONG MUST WOMEN WAIT

The Women's Suffrage Movement: 1920

The women's suffrage movement was the decades-long fight for women's right to vote. The movement began in 1848 with the Seneca Falls Convention, the first women's rights convention, and the first suffrage organizations were created in 1869. But in the early 1900s, few states allowed women to vote. Over the years, women's organizations worked tirelessly to advance women's voting rights by lobbying governments, petitioning, organizing, and holding public demonstrations.

In the 20th century, the National Woman's Party (NWP), led by an activist named Alice Paul, organized attention-getting activities such as hunger strikes and White House pickets. Paul was a vocal advocate of women's rights and encouraged protests and large rallies. Paul had a confrontational style that helped draw in a younger population of women to fight for women's rights.

The National American Woman Suffrage Association (NAWSA), led by Carrie Chapman Catt, took a more moderate approach. It focused on campaigns to grant women the right to vote in national and state elections. During World War I, for example, Catt organized a drive that linked women's right to vote to the war

effort. Because it displayed patriotism, the campaign was able to gain support. While the men went overseas to fight, the women took jobs. The country saw that women were not only just as patriotic as men, but also as willing and capable as them. The effort worked. President Woodrow Wilson declared his support for women to vote.

On August 18, 1920, the 19th Amendment to the Constitution was ratified. This amendment guaranteed the right to vote to all US citizens regardless of sex. This was the pinnacle of the women's suffrage movement. On November 2, 1920, more than eight million women voted in elections for the first time across the entire United States.

SUFFRAGE PARADES

The first suffrage parade was organized by the Women's Political Union in 1910. The parade, attended by a couple hundred people, was held in New York City as a way to gain attention and publicity for the movement. By 1912, more than 20,000 supporters attended another suffrage parade in New York City. The first parade organized by the NAWSA was held in 1913 in Washington, DC.

CHAPTER TWO

1921 TO 1940

The period following World War I brought political and social changes that had major impact on the United States. Americans were happy to be out of the war, and they looked forward to things returning to normal. With the victory, there was a renewed positive spirit prevailing. People now wanted to find outlets to relax.

Modern forms of entertainment became popular. Musicians, artists, and writers pushed the boundaries of their genres. Sports, especially baseball, became a favorite pastime. And, beginning in 1920, radio broadcasts made it possible for people to enjoy concerts, shows, and games at home when they couldn't be there in person. Advancements in air travel also played a major role during this time: Charles Lindbergh became the first person to make a nonstop flight from New York to Paris. Amelia Earhart became the first woman to make the same flight. And automobiles and modern household appliances made everyday life easier.

But all the good times came with a price. The economy grew very quickly and finally crashed when it could not keep up with consumers borrowing money, and the stock market fell. The United States experienced a Great Depression, and it would take a New Deal in order to recover.

Flappers dancing in the snow in 1926

The Roaring Twenties: 1920s

In the years following World War I, Americans hoped for a return to life as it was before. Driven by a boom in construction, purchases of new cars and large appliances, as well as easy **credit** to afford it all, the 1920s was a time of continuous change and growth.

During this time, jazz music became very popular. Music clubs and nightclubs opened across the United States, giving people a chance to enjoy themselves.

Women moved into new roles and jobs as well. They were voting, earning college degrees, and many moved to the cities to live and work on their own.

MEET LOUIS ARMSTRONG

Louis Armstrong was a trumpet player, composer, and singer who changed how music was played: he improvised. He wasn't content to stick to the set melody. Instead, he introduced and recorded a solo style that reflected his fun-loving personality. Armstrong also sang on these records. It was a new style of singing called "scat singing." Scat uses nonsense syllables and sounds in the place of words, making a voice sound like a musical instrument. Most of the time, the scat singing would follow the melody being played, and sometimes it sounded like the singer just forgot the words to the song even though it was intentional.

Women's fashion also began to change during this time period. They began wearing their hair shorter. Long dresses shortened, and some dresses were even sleeveless. Women who wore these dresses were called **flappers**.

Automobiles became popular during the 1920s. More cars meant more demand, so the automobile industry began a system of **mass production** to get cars through the production line quicker. With more cars on the road, the number of gas stations, motels, highways, and diners increased as people traveled.

Cities grew and new technologies sprang up with them. Vacuum cleaners, refrigerators, washing machines, and electric stoves were made affordable during this time, so many families were able to purchase them to make daily housework a little more manageable. Radios and telephones became more common and helped people stay connected.

People were enjoying themselves and spending money. But not everyone had cash to cover their spending and they began to buy things on credit. Although the 1920s started with a roar, the constant spending eventually led to economic problems by the end of the decade.

FORD AUTOMOBILES

Henry Ford, businessman and founder of the Ford Motor Company, forever changed how goods were produced when he introduced the assembly line. In his factory, each worker was assigned a certain task, and cars were assembled as they moved past each person on a conveyor belt. By using the assembly line, the time it took to make an automobile dropped from 12 hours to two-and-a-half hours.

Charles Lindbergh in 1923

Charles Lindbergh's Flight: 1927

In 1919, a hotel owner in New York City offered a $25,000 prize to the first person to fly nonstop from New York to Paris, France. Up to that point, no one had been able to make the flight, and some pilots even died trying. By 1927, the prize still had not been claimed. A young pilot named Charles Lindbergh heard about the prize money and wanted to win it.

On May 20, 1927, Lindbergh accepted the challenge. He took off from Roosevelt Field in Long Island, New York, flying a single-engine airplane named the *Spirit of St. Louis*. He crossed the Atlantic

Raymond Orteig was a French-American hotel owner, philanthropist, and aviation enthusiast. He was responsible for funding the $25,000 Orteig Prize in 1919 that inspired Charles Lindbergh to make the first nonstop flight from New York to Paris. Orteig originally made the prize available for five years. But when no one had claimed it, he offered it again. When Lindbergh made the journey, Orteig met him in France to congratulate him. Orteig's prize and Lindbergh's flight inspired others to offer rewards promoting advancements in aviation.

Ocean safely and landed at Le Bourget Field near Paris. Lindbergh's flight was approximately 33½ hours long, a distance of 3,600 miles. He had made the first **transatlantic flight**. When he landed at Le Bourget Field, approximately 100,000 people were there to witness aviation history.

Lindbergh instantly became a public figure and was greeted and cheered wherever he went. He received the first-ever Distinguished Flying Cross medal and the Congressional Medal of Honor from President Calvin Coolidge. And Lindbergh flew his *Spirit of St. Louis* around the United

States, giving speeches that promoted the field of aviation. Within 10 years of his first transatlantic flight, passenger airline travel was established throughout the United States.

The *Spirit of St. Louis*, the airplane that Lindbergh flew from New York to Paris, was a single-engine monoplane, meaning it had one pair of wings. Under normal circumstances, the plane could seat five people. For Lindbergh's historic flight, however, extra fuel tanks replaced the seats, so the flight could be nonstop. Its top speed was 120 miles per hour.

Babe Ruth (right)
autographs a bat

Babe Ruth's Home Run Record: 1927

Known as the "the Sultan of Swat" and "the Great Bambino," Babe Ruth became a household name in the 1920s for his baseball achievements. In those years, games were broadcast on the radio with the announcer describing, play by play, what was happening on the field. For those who could go to the stadium, the games were even more exciting.

Ruth played most of his career for the New York Yankees and helped the Yankees win four World Series titles. Fans flocked to the stadiums to see him play. Everyone wanted to see him swing the bat.

In 1921, Ruth hit a record 59 home runs—a record that still stood in 1927. During the 1927 season, Ruth led the league in home runs, as he often did. As the season wore on, Ruth continued to outperform, surprising fans by hitting 16 home runs during the month of September alone.

On September 29, 1927, he tied his 1921 record. On September 30, with just one game left in the season, Babe Ruth stepped up to the plate against a left-handed Washington Senators pitcher named Tom Zachary. In the eighth inning, Ruth launched the ball high into the right-field bleachers. As he began a slow stroll around the bases, the crowd celebrated with a roar. Babe Ruth had hit his 60th home

MEET TOM ZACHARY

Tom Zachary was a Major League Baseball pitcher who played from 1918 until 1936. He logged 186 victories, appearing for seven different teams before he retired. Over his career, he earned two World Series championship rings and is credited with a perfect record (12–0) in the 1929 season. Nonetheless, Zachary is probably best known for pitching the fastball that Babe Ruth hit into right field to break his home run record in 1927.

run in the last game of the season, breaking his own home run record. His home run record stood for 40 years.

BASEBALL ON THE RADIO

The first baseball game broadcast on the radio was on August 5, 1921, on KDKA in Pittsburgh, Pennsylvania. The announcer was Harold Arlin. The first World Series broadcast was also broadcast in 1921 with Tommy Cowan commentating. Soon, more broadcasters were announcing games, and radio began to bring baseball into homes across America.

Comedy duo Laurel and Hardy in 1928

The Big Screen Comes to Life: 1927

When audiences first heard actor Al Jolson say, "You ain't heard nothing yet," they gasped and clapped in delight. Silent films had been around since 1903, but in 1927, a new era of movies was born. Those first movies were called "talkies." The first feature-length American film with dialogue and singing was *The Jazz Singer*, directed by Alan Crosland. This new kind of movie helped Warner Bros. Pictures become recognized as a major studio and earned them awards and honors.

Walt Disney was an American animator, film producer, and entrepreneur. Born in Chicago in 1901, he moved to California in the early 1920s and set up Disney Brothers Studio with his brother, Roy. Walt was a pioneer in animation and is probably best known for his creation of the cartoon character Mickey Mouse. Mickey Mouse became an iconic symbol recognized around the world. Disney later expanded from films into amusement parks, including Disneyland in California and Walt Disney World in Florida, giving fans places to celebrate Mickey Mouse and many other Disney characters.

Lights of New York, released a year later in 1928, became the first feature produced by Warner Bros. to have all the dialogue recorded. Seeing the success Warner Bros. had with *The Jazz Singer,* other studios began to invest money to wire their theaters for sound. This paved the way for the transition from silent movies to full-sound movies.

In 1928, the first animated short cartoon with voices appeared on a screen in New York. It was Walt Disney's *Steamboat Willie,* featuring Mickey Mouse. It was an instant hit, so within a couple of months, Disney created a series of cartoons with Mickey Mouse. One of the animated movies that followed was *Plane Crazy*, where Mickey played the character of Charles Lindbergh. This animated series launched Mickey Mouse into homes and hearts across the country. Walt Disney began marketing Mickey Mouse and started a fan club called the Mickey Mouse Club.

VITAPHONE

Vitaphone was the name of the film sound system developed by Warner Bros. that gave sound to silent films. In the years before the first talkie, the films had only a musical score. There were approximately 200 films using Vitaphone features prior to *The Jazz Singer*, but none of them were full-length films.

A soup kitchen in 1931

The Great Depression:
1929–1930s

All the fun of the 1920s had many Americans feeling good about the economy, but they did not know how quickly things were about to go bad. October 24, 1929, is known as "Black Thursday" because that was the day of the Wall Street Crash of 1929.

In the 1920s, people had borrowed money from local banks to buy stocks offered by companies. (Selling stocks, or shares, is a way for a company to raise money to cover its expenses. In return, the company pays these shareholders a portion of future profits.) But when the shareholders could not pay back the loans, the banks began to run out of money, causing

MEET PRESIDENT HERBERT HOOVER

Herbert Hoover was the 31st president of the United States; he served from 1929 to 1933. When he became president, the economy was doing great, but the stock market crash sent the economy into a depression. His stance was Americans should not go cold and hungry, but he also believed the federal government should not get involved. He left it up to local governments to help. Hoover lost the 1932 presidential election since many blamed him for the lingering effects of the Great Depression.

them to collapse. As the loans became worthless, the company stocks became worthless. Then, as the stock prices plummeted, the companies themselves became worthless and went out of business. Many people found themselves out of work and out of money. All these problems set off what's known as the Great Depression, the longest period of unemployment and low economic activity in the 20th century.

Americans were without jobs, and many were hungry and some became homeless. Approximately 75 percent of American families were living in poverty. The divide between the rich and poor grew tremendously. Factory workers became unemployed and could no longer afford groceries, and farmers could not earn enough money to keep the farms operating. Then, the country experienced an extreme drought in the Great Plains region. High winds blew away acres of soil in this region, creating what became known as the Dust Bowl.

President Herbert Hoover did not believe the government should fund relief programs to help struggling Americans. He felt that things would improve if people regained confidence in the economy, so he put his focus on strengthening it. This did not help. Unemployment and homelessness continued to grow, and by 1932, those who were homeless began to build makeshift homes out of scraps and boxes. These were called "Hoovervilles."

SOUP KITCHENS

Soup kitchens were started by churches and other groups who wanted to help feed those desperate for food during the Great Depression. They gave away food from the government and from donations from people in the community who grew food in their gardens. For some Americans, the soup kitchen was the only way they could eat each day.

FDR signs the
Social Security
Act in 1935

The New Deal: 1933–1939

When Franklin D. Roosevelt took office in 1933 as president of the United States, the country was suffering from the Great Depression and had the highest unemployment numbers ever. Roosevelt, known as FDR, had run his campaign on a promise to Americans for a "New Deal" where he would use the government to create jobs. During his first 100 days in office, Roosevelt set up many new agencies to combat unemployment.

Some of the agencies that were established hired workers to construct roads, dams, parks, and new buildings across the country. Others regulated businesses, farming, banking, the labor industry, and the stock market. FDR also implemented a

Eleanor Roosevelt was President Roosevelt's wife. She played a major role during FDR's presidency because she traveled the country, talked to people, saw what conditions were like, and then reported all she learned to him. She became an advocate for the poor, minorities, and the disadvantaged. Eleanor was also the first First Lady to hold her own press conferences. She only allowed women reporters to be present, because she wanted to make sure that women reporters wouldn't lose their jobs.

several-days-long bank holiday. This meant people were unable to withdraw their cash in a panic; the bank holiday was meant to calm them down.

After the holiday, the president convinced Americans to start putting their savings back into banks. Slowly, the banks became stronger; those that were not stable closed for good. An important program that came out of the New Deal was the Federal Deposit and Insurance Corporation (FDIC). It insures bank deposits and protects people's money up to a certain dollar amount per account.

The follow-up stage of FDR's program was called the Second New Deal, which began in 1935. The Works Progress Administration (WPA) employed people to construct highways, buildings, libraries, schools, hospitals, parks, and bridges. It also paid artists to create murals, sculptures, and plays. FDR wanted to protect workers, so the National Labor Relations Act (NLRA) was passed in 1935. It banned unfair workplace practices and gave unions the right to strike and bargain. The Fair Labor Standards Act of 1938 guaranteed workers a minimum wage, overtime pay, and banned child labor.

Roosevelt's list of agencies and laws is often referred to as "alphabet soup" because of their initials used to represent the agency or program. Some include the TVA (Tennessee Valley Authority), CCC (Civilian Conservation Corps), SSA (Social Security Act), NYA (National Youth Administration), and FHA (Federal Housing Administration). The New Deal's programs helped provide jobs, feed Americans, and make lasting improvements all across the United States.

THE TENNESSEE VALLEY AUTHORITY

The Tennessee Valley Authority employed workers to build dams, preserve forests, and bring electricity to rural areas along the Tennessee River. For the first time some homes and farms in the rural south had access to electricity.

CHAPTER THREE

1941 TO 1960

When the 1940s arrived, the United States was focused on the home front, still recovering from the economic slump it was in from the Great Depression. But a new wave of world events was emerging on the horizon. People watched as tensions were building in Europe—the continent was again headed for war.

The war brought new alliances as countries saw the value in aligning themselves with others with similar goals. Pacts were made and treaties were signed that would last for many decades. The United States found itself in a new kind of competition, one that was heating up with every passing second.

The 1950s introduced a postwar boom in America, and new avenues opened for a younger generation to explore. The economy had recovered, and finances were better for most. People were moving to the suburbs and having children, popular culture took on new fads, and new technologies were introduced that made an enormous impact on lifestyle.

At the same time, Americans began to speak out against inequality and injustice. This led to the beginnings of the civil rights movement.

The invasion of Normandy in 1944

World War II: 1940–1945

It was just two decades after World War I ended, and the world was not prepared for the conflict brewing in Europe. There had been political instability and economic devastation in Europe following World War I. There was a worldwide economic depression. People were experiencing high **inflation** and unemployment, and **fascism** was on the rise. All these factors set the stage for another world war.

Adolf Hitler was a fascist dictator of Germany. He teamed up with fascist Benito Mussolini of Italy, and the two leaders proclaimed that world power would "rotate" on a Berlin-Rome axis. Later, Emperor Hirohito of Japan joined them, and the three became known as the Axis Powers. As these countries formed their alliances, several others began to get nervous about their intentions. The other countries came to be known as the Allies, or Allied Powers, and included Great Britain, the Soviet Union, France, Poland, China, and the United States.

When Hitler invaded Poland in 1939, Great Britain and France declared war on Germany. World War II had begun. Initially, the US Congress wanted nothing to do with the conflict in Europe. But that changed when Pearl Harbor, a US naval base in Hawaii, was attacked by Japan on December 7, 1941. The United States declared war on Japan and entered World War II.

American civilians made sacrifices for the war effort. People had to begin **rationing** scarce

MEET ROSIE THE RIVETER

The character of Rosie the Riveter became an iconic symbol appearing on government posters during World War II. It encouraged women to help in the war effort on the home front. This fictional character showed a strong woman working a factory job. Almost one out of every four women worked outside of the home, and between 1940 and 1945, the number of female workers in the country increased by 10 percent.

items as factories and businesses turned their production to supplying the soldiers with equipment. Women went to work in factories and shipyards and joined the military. Black Americans also began to take on different roles. One group, known as the Tuskegee Airmen, was composed of elite Black American pilots who flew over Europe.

Americans found themselves facing the Japanese threat in the Pacific islands, while facing German and Italian threats in Europe and northern Africa. Germany eventually surrendered to the Allied Powers on May 8, 1945, followed by Japan's surrender later that summer.

World War II was the deadliest military conflict in history. Nearly 3 percent of the world's population lost their lives, including the victims of the Holocaust, which claimed about two-thirds of Europe's Jewish population.

THE HOLOCAUST

The Holocaust was the systematic state-sponsored killing of Jewish men, women, and children, as well as millions of other "undesirables," by Nazi Germany. Hitler planned to get rid of all Jewish people in Europe. Some six million Jews perished because of it.

Winston Churchill
and Dwight
Eisenhower in 1950

The Push for Peace: 1940s

At the end of World War II, the United States and
the Soviet Union emerged as two global superpowers. The war had left the United States in a position
where isolationism was no longer an option. The
United States had played a major role in defeating
fascism, and it wanted to be sure that democracy
remained strong in Europe. Meanwhile, the Soviet
Union's presence in Europe was also important. The
Soviets believed, however, that their political system
of **communism** was just as necessary.

When Germany was finally defeated, the Allied
Powers had to decide what to do with the war-torn
country. Ultimately, they decided to divide the country

in half—East Germany was controlled by the Soviet Union, and West Germany was controlled by the Allies. The division of East Germany and West Germany led to issues, however. West Germany began to thrive as industries were rebuilt. But those in East Germany struggled as the communist control of the Soviet Union held them back. This led British Prime Minister Winston Churchill to state that an "iron curtain" had fallen across Europe. By this he meant that the Soviet Union, under its leader Joseph Stalin, had cut Eastern Europe off from the rest of the world.

The United States and its allies in Europe were wary of the Soviet Union's goals. On

MEET HARRY S. TRUMAN

Harry S. Truman became the 33rd president of the United States on April 12, 1945. During his time in office, he had to make some difficult decisions. During World War II, he gave the order for atomic bombs to be dropped on two Japanese cities, Hiroshima and Nagasaki. Several years later, he was part of the negotiations of the North Atlantic Treaty Organization. And when North Korea invaded South Korea in 1950, just a few years after the end of World War II, he reluctantly sent troops to defend the south from the communist north.

April 4, 1949, the United States and 11 other nations signed the North Atlantic Treaty, creating the North Atlantic Treaty Organization (NATO). The treaty stated that all nations would help one another in the event of a military attack. It also stated that NATO members were joined by a community of values promoting individual liberty, human rights, democracy, and the rule of the law.

The NATO agreement pleased many Americans, who wanted to remain isolationist. Though the countries were bound to protect each other, each country could choose when to assist the others without an automatic declaration of war or obligation to commit to it.

UNITED NATIONS

Founded in 1945, the United Nations (UN) is an international organization, headquartered in New York City. The purpose of the UN is to solve international problems and take action on issues confronting humanity, such as peace, security, climate change, human rights, terrorism, and health emergencies. The UN has provided a means for governments to find ways to solve problems together.

The Berlin Wall in 1961

The Cold War: From 1947

Beginning in 1947, the United States and the Soviet Union, along with their allies, were in a long conflict that came to be known as the Cold War. Although technically no actual fighting occurred, this time period is marked by a hostile nuclear arms race and the desire to dominate the globe.

Relations between the United States and the Soviet Union gradually became tense after the end of World War II. Americans were so concerned about the spread of communism that they even began to fear that communist spies might be living in the United States. Joseph McCarthy, a senator from Wisconsin, accused state department officials—as well as some famous actors and artists—of being communists. He could not prove his accusations, but he succeeded in ruining the reputations of many people.

The mistrust in each other caused the two countries to begin stockpiling weapons and missiles in case they were needed for a future war. Both sides had nuclear technology, and by 1962, both the United States and the Soviet Union had built missile defenses pointed at one another. The Cold War was anything but friendly as it set both sides ready to fight at a moment's notice.

Over the years, several proxy wars took place as the two superpowers jockeyed for position. A "proxy war" is a conflict where the two sides don't get

MEET SENATOR JOSEPH MCCARTHY

Senator Joseph McCarthy tried to convince Americans that communist spies were in the US government. He made very persuasive accusations, and many people did not question or speak out against him. When he accused the US Army of having spies, however, public opinion began to turn against him. He lost his credibility when the Army–McCarthy hearings were televised, leading to a formal condemnation, called a censure, by Congress.

directly involved, but support other foes. The Cuban Missile Crisis, the Korean War, the Vietnam War, and even the space race, which began in the 1950s, were proxy wars that allowed the United States and the Soviet Union to be engaged financially or to fight against a communist or capitalist force.

Although President Richard Nixon took steps in the early 1970s to implement a new approach to international relations, when President Ronald Reagan took office, three presidents later, the Cold War still did not look like it was going to end. Nearly four decades would pass before Soviet President Mikhail Gorbachev introduced two policies in 1985 that reexamined Russia's relationship with the rest of the world and led to the end of the Cold War.

THE BERLIN WALL

Just like Germany was divided, the capital city of Berlin was divided into East Berlin and West Berlin. At first, people could travel across the border. But, when many people from East Berlin began to move to West Berlin seeking better living conditions and opportunities, the Soviets became angry. They constructed a wall to separate East Berlin from West Berlin. This became known as the Berlin Wall.

A combat operation during the Korean War in 1951

The Korean War: 1950–1953

At the end of World War II, the Allied Powers divided the Korean peninsula into two halves, forming two new nations: North Korea and South Korea. North Korea was the territory north of the 38th parallel—the boundary between Soviet and American occupation zones. This part became a communist country. South Korea was the territory of Korea south of the 38th parallel.

Conflict began on June 25, 1950, when soldiers from the Korean People's Army invaded South Korea. The United States saw this invasion as a way communism could take over the world. In an effort to

General Douglas MacArthur served in the United States Army during World War II and the Korean War. He led the American coalition of United Nations troops during the beginning of the Korean War. While President Truman wanted a limited war in Southeast Asia, MacArthur called for a more aggressive presence. General MacArthur was eventually removed from his command for being insubordinate. He later returned to the United States and was welcomed and honored as a hero.

prevent the spread of communism, President Harry S. Truman sent US troops to help South Korea.

A year after fighting, peace talks began at Panmunjom, a village just north of the border between the two Koreas. Although negotiations were ongoing, fighting still continued. The talks stalled as there were some parts of the agreement that both sides simply could not agree upon. Finally, on July 27, 1953, the Korean Armistice Agreement was signed. In this agreement, South Korea gained an extra 1,500 square miles of territory and a two-mile-wide Korean

Demilitarized Zone was created. However, no peace treaty has ever been signed. The two Koreas are technically still at war, although they aren't fighting.

THE 38TH PARALLEL

The 38th parallel is the line of latitude that marks the boundary between North and South Korea. It was initially chosen by US military planners in July 1945 as an army boundary at the end of World War II. It was intended as a temporary division of the country of Korea, but with the onset of the Cold War, it became permanent.

Apollo 11 in 1969

The Space Race Takes Off: 1950s

3...2...1...Blast off! It was a race to outer space. Countries were trying to see who was going to earn the bragging rights of making it to space first. During this time, the space race was born and many advances in the fields of space and aeronautics were made.

The two countries vying for those bragging rights were the United States and the Soviet Union. Many refer to the space race as another Cold War competition to see who could outshine and outperform the other.

With the launch of the first Earth satellite, *Sputnik I*, in 1957, the Soviet Union took the driver's seat. The United States quickly followed up in 1958 when the National Aeronautics and Space Administration (NASA) was created to develop civilian aerospace research. Further, the National Defense Education Act was passed in that same year. This gave more federal funding for math and science education.

MEET PRESIDENT DWIGHT D. EISENHOWER

Dwight D. Eisenhower was the 34th president of the United States. He served from 1953 to 1961. In 1958, he signed the National Aeronautics and Space Act, creating NASA. This agency was dedicated to space exploration and research. He also created two national security space agencies to operate alongside NASA's program. One agency looked at the military potential of space; the second used orbiting satellites to gather intelligence on the Soviet Union and its allies.

In 1961, the Soviet Union sent the first man into space. This put more pressure on the United States, and President John F. Kennedy committed to landing a man on the Moon by the end of the decade. The Apollo program, also known as Project Apollo, was dedicated to this goal, and the United States had a plan to make this mission happen.

Many technological advancements

were made during the early years of the space race that still have an impact on our lives today—satellites improved our communications, navigation and weather forecasting were redesigned, and the first cordless tools were developed.

SPUTNIK I

Sputnik I was launched on October 4, 1957, by the Soviet Union. It was the first artificial satellite and man-made object to be placed into Earth's orbit. The satellite was launched using an intercontinental ballistic missile. It broadcast information back to Earth for three weeks before its batteries died. It then fell back into the atmosphere two months later.

A supermarket in 1957

The Fifties: 1950s

Rock and roll, television, and movies set the stage for the 1950s to be a fabulous time for fun and entertainment. The war effort spurred manufacturing, and with it came jobs and prosperity. Americans had more money to spend than ever before and more leisure time to enjoy popular culture all around them.

Rock and roll was new on the music scene. This type of music centered on themes of love and rebellion, both of which appealed to teenagers. Musicians such as Fats Domino, Chuck Berry, and Elvis Presley combined rhythm and blues, soul, and gospel to popularize a brand-new kind of music.

Elvis Presley became a sensation during the 1950s as both a musician and actor. He is one of the biggest names in rock and roll history, and his dance moves were like no one else's. His first big hit was a song titled "Heartbreak Hotel," and in 1956, he starred in the movie *Love Me Tender*, expanding his fame from singing into acting. His presence on the stage helped rock and roll become popular. During his career, he had 18 number one singles.

Television shows began to compete with movies. Although TV was not new, only a small percentage of Americans could afford them prior to the 1950s. With more money in their pockets, Americans began to purchase consumer goods such as televisions. And with this popularity came a range of shows, from family shows to Westerns to programs just for children.

Television changed the way Americans saw the world.

Although the 1950s saw many fabulous and fun things in the areas of consumerism, there was growing agitation around civil rights, especially in the South. The old Jim Crow laws were being questioned on a wider scale, and Black Americans were loudly asking why they were treated differently. As the decade drew to a close, the idea of "separate but equal" was put to the test in more than just public schools, and segregation began to unravel in the late 1950s.

COLOR TELEVISION

Although the first televisions appeared as early as the late 1920s, television sets were expensive and rare, and the picture was in black and white. Color television changed the way viewers saw the world during the 1950s. Color television displayed a sense of realism and life that was not seen with black-and-white television sets. Viewers could see the world the way it actually appeared.

CHAPTER FOUR

1961 TO 1980

In the 1960s, the civil rights movement that had begun in the 1940s was in full effect. Black Americans and their white allies were fighting for freedoms and rights long denied to them.

The United States was also once again engaged in a war on foreign soil, this time in Vietnam. Meanwhile, a new counterculture was taking place and some Americans were embracing an alternative lifestyle. The new freedoms and liberties saw women begin to demand more opportunities and equal pay through the Women's Liberation Movement. Then, at the end of the 1970s, American citizens were taken hostage in Iran, which would impact the United States' position in the Middle East for decades to come.

Civil rights march in 1963

The Civil Rights Movement: 1960s

The doctrine of "separate but equal" was declared unconstitutional in 1954 by the Supreme Court in a landmark legal case called *Brown v. Board of Education.* This court case, followed a year later by the Montgomery Bus Boycott, set off a chain reaction that became the civil rights movement in the United States. During this time, Black Americans and sympathetic white people protested against racial segregation and discrimination in the United States. This movement had been coming for a long time, but it finally gained the momentum it needed to see real change.

Martin Luther King Jr. emerged as the leader of the civil rights movement when he led the Montgomery Bus Boycott in 1955. Later, he was instrumental in creating the Southern Christian Leadership Conference, a group organized to promote nonviolent protests against discrimination. During the March on Washington in 1963, King's speech emphasized his hope and belief that someday all people would be seen as equal.

The protesters staged sit-ins, boycotts, and marches as ways to display the urgency for social change and justice nonviolently. The Freedom Riders of 1961 were activists who rode interstate buses in an effort to desegregate Southern bus terminals. In 1963, Martin Luther King Jr., wrote his "Letter from a Birmingham Jail," where he warned that Black Americans might one day become so frustrated that they would turn to Black nationalism, and it would make racial tensions even more difficult. On August 28, 1963, at one of the biggest protests—the March on Washington—King delivered his now-famous "I Have a Dream" speech, where he described civil rights goals and the privileges all Americans deserved: "life, liberty, and the pursuit of happiness."

The impact of the civil rights movement in the United States was significant. It helped pave the way for many advances for Black Americans during this time. One of the greatest achievements was the Civil Rights Act of 1964, which prohibited discrimination based on color, race, or religion. This gave all people the right to go to public places and not be forced to sit in certain sections based on race.

NATIONAL ASSOCIATION FOR THE ADVANCEMENT OF COLORED PEOPLE

The NAACP is the nation's largest and most recognized civil rights organization. During the _Brown v. Board of Education_ case, the NAACP Legal Defense and Educational Fund served as the attorneys bringing the case before the Supreme Court. This case helped desegregate public schools. The NAACP also helped advance the passage of the Civil Rights Act of 1964 and the Voting Rights Act of 1965, both of which were important milestones in granting equal rights to Black Americans.

A battle during the Vietnam War in 1965

The United States in the Vietnam War: 1961–1973

In 1954, Vietnam was divided into North Vietnam and South Vietnam. North Vietnam was ruled by a communist government, but South Vietnam was controlled by a government friendly to the United States. The communists wanted to reunite the country by taking over South Vietnam.

In 1961, President John F. Kennedy sent a team to report on the worsening conditions in South Vietnam. The purpose of the report was to see if the United States should build up the American military there and send economic and technical help.

Lyndon B. Johnson became the 36th president of the United States on November 22, 1963, following the assassination of John F. Kennedy. As president, Johnson declared a "war on poverty." His vision for the American people was called "A Great Society." His stance on foreign policy was much like those who came before him—he worried about the spread of communism around the world. He sent more troops into Vietnam. When it was time to seek reelection, he chose not to run.

The US policy was based on a "Domino Theory"—if South Vietnam became a communist nation, then all of Southeast Asia would fall under communist control. With this theory in mind, the United States increased US aid and advice. Kennedy authorized sending troops to Vietnam in 1961.

But Americans were divided over whether the country should get involved or leave it up to Vietnam to settle. Protesters marched in the streets in order to let their voices be heard. Those who did not agree with the fighting joined a lifestyle called the counterculture, and its members were called hippies.

Many American lives were lost in the jungles of Vietnam. The North Vietnamese military was called the Vietcong. They knew the jungles and land well, making fighting the war more difficult for the American troops. US President Richard Nixon agreed to a ceasefire, hoping to end the conflict. But after the United States pulled its troops out of South Vietnam, North Vietnam took over. Today, it is one country led by communist rule.

GULF OF TONKIN INCIDENT

The Gulf of Tonkin incident on August 4, 1964, is on record as North Vietnamese ships attacking an American vessel. Though the US ship involved, the *USS Maddox*, fired its weapons as a warning, subsequent reports of the incident revealed no evidence of an attack. President Johnson nonetheless responded by ordering controversial attacks on North Vietnamese targets.

Anti-war protestors in 1972

The Counterculture:
1960s–1970s

Peace, love, and music characterized a new movement in the 1960s. This movement became known as the counterculture, and its members, hippies, were mostly young people who had long hair and wore loose, colorful clothing. Many turned their backs on the standard American culture from their parents' days and formed their own ideas and values.

The hippie counterculture reached its height during America's involvement in the Vietnam War. This group believed the United States should not fight in a war if there was no direct threat to

American safety. Since the war was being fought overseas, they did not see a reason to continue to send more US troops.

One lasting impact from the 1960s counterculture involved the American diet. Hippies turned to natural foods and supported living off the land. Health food stores began to sell such foods as wheat germ, granola, yogurt, and organic meats and vegetables. Eating a vegetarian diet also became popular during this time. Eating from local establishments was important.

Some hippies chose to maintain this alternative lifestyle as they grew older, but others eventually rejoined society. Although the hippie counterculture movement ended, some ideas that emerged during that time are still around today, such as solar panels—hippie

MEET JOAN BAEZ

A singer, songwriter, and activist, Joan Baez blazed a trail for herself during the counterculture of the 1960s. Baez used her music to express both social and political causes, and she used her fame as a voice for change. At the March on Washington in 1963, Baez sang the gospel song "We Shall Overcome," which later became a Top-40 hit and an anthem of the civil rights movement.

communes were the first to use solar energy—and the emphasis on organic foods.

WOODSTOCK

In 1969, one of the largest and most famous music celebrations ever was held on a dairy farm in upstate New York. The Woodstock music festival took place over three days and featured 32 bands. Some of the legendary performers included the Grateful Dead, Jimi Hendrix, Janis Joplin, Joan Baez, the Who, Jefferson Airplane, and Creedence Clearwater Revival. More than 400,000 people attended the music festival.

A women's liberation march in 1971

The Women's Liberation Movement: 1960s–1970s

During the 1960s and 1970s, the Women's Liberation Movement fought for equal rights and opportunities for women. The movement was wide-ranging and extended into many areas of a woman's life such as work, family, and politics.

When the US Congress passed the Equal Pay Act of 1963, it promised equal pay and wages for the same work regardless of sex, race, religion, or national origin. If women were doing the same work as men, they should be fairly compensated for their labor. Unfortunately, the act was hard to enforce, and

MEET BETTY FRIEDAN

Author Betty Friedan published *The Feminine Mystique* in 1963. In the book, she wrote about the mind of a suburban housewife who seems to have it all, but in reality is deadened by domestic life. Friedan's book became a bestseller and opened many women's eyes to their situation in society. It provided an important spark that ignited the Women's Liberation Movement.

even today, women usually earn about 20 percent less than men; it is known as the "gender gap."

The Civil Rights Act of 1964 included language, in Title VII, that prohibited employment discrimination on the basis of sex, race, religion, or national origin.

In 1972, Congress passed Title IX of the Higher Education Act. This prohibited discrimination on the basis of sex in any educational program receiving federal funds. This forced all-male public schools to open their doors to women, and athletic programs to sponsor and finance female sports teams. These laws are still in effect today in schools across the United States.

While the first wave of feminism focused on women's right to vote in the 1920s, a second wave grew in intensity in the 1960s. The National Organization for Women (NOW), for instance, was created in 1966 to apply national pressure for some of their topics. At first, the organization had a hard time getting off the ground because the members didn't always agree on issues that were controversial. The conservative and liberal members were often at odds. Nonetheless, over time, the Women's Liberation Movement made many strides in important areas, such as full equality in the military and funding for childcare.

EQUAL RIGHTS AMENDMENT

One main goal of the National Organization for Women was the passage of the Equal Rights Amendment (ERA) to the US Constitution. The goal of the amendment was to further guarantee equal rights for women. The amendment was originally proposed in 1923 but didn't find full support until the 1960s. It was passed by Congress in 1972, but failed to receive the 38 state ratifications it needed to become part of the Constitution before the time limit expired.

Astronaut Gene Cernan on the Moon in 1972

The First Man on the Moon: 1969

The space race began in the late 1950s, and the Soviet Union made the first move when it sent a man into orbit around the Earth. In 1961, President John F. Kennedy announced the goal of sending Americans to the Moon.

With the stage set for some intense competition, both the United States and the Soviet Union were taking steps to "out space" each other. President Kennedy increased the budget for the National Aeronautics and Space Administration (NASA). With this increased budget, the Apollo

Born in Ohio, Neil Armstrong showed a love for flying at a young age. By 16, he had earned his aviation license. He graduated from Purdue University with a degree in aeronautical engineering and went to work for NASA as a test pilot and engineer. Later, he joined the astronaut program. Armstrong had his first mission to space in 1966, serving as the command pilot. He is best known for being the first man to walk on the Moon.

program—dedicated to going to the Moon—was created, and NASA scientists worked around the clock to come up with advancements in aeronautics and space.

Apollo 11 took off from Kennedy Space Center on July 16, 1969. It traveled 240,000 miles before entering the lunar orbit on July 19. The next day, the lunar module *Eagle* separated from the command module and started its descent to the Moon's surface. On July 20, 1969, Neil Armstrong and Buzz Aldrin became the first two American astronauts to ever land on the surface of the Moon. Armstrong then became the first person to walk on the Moon. During his first step, he is remembered as saying, "That's one small step for man, one giant leap for mankind." With the Moon landing and moon walk, the United States won first place in the space race.

The *Eagle* was the name of the Lunar Module used during the Apollo 11 moon landing. It was used for the descent to the Moon's surface and served as a home base when the astronauts were on the Moon. The astronauts slept aboard the *Eagle* for one night on the Moon before making their way back to the command module.

The Iranian hostage crisis in 1979

The Iran Embassy Takeover and Hostage Crisis: 1979

The Shah of Iran had come to power in the early 1950s with the aid of British and American covert forces who helped to stage a military takeover. The former government had been democratically elected, but the Shah installed himself as a monarch. Even though he instituted many reforms, people were unhappy because he tried to do away with their traditions—he wanted to Westernize the country. Further, his secret police committed many atrocities. The people of Iran blamed the United States

Mohammed Reza Pahlavi was the last Shah of Iran. ("Shah" means monarch or king.) He served from 1941 until 1979. He became Shah when a military coup overthrew Mohammad Mossadegh, the elected prime minister. The Shah had a pro-Western foreign policy and encouraged economic development in Iran. His people were dissatisfied with him because some thought the country's oil wealth was not distributed evenly, his secret police were brutal, and his Western influences were not in line with their beliefs.

for interfering in their country.

After the Iranian Revolution in 1979, the Shah was ousted and sent into exile. Later that year, US President Jimmy Carter allowed the Shah to come to the United States for medical treatment. This further angered the Iranian people, who wanted the Shah returned to face trial, but the United States refused to return him.

On November 4, 1979, a group of Iranian college students took over the US embassy in Tehran, the capital city. For 444 days, the students held 52 Americans hostage.

Although President Carter tried to end the hostage crisis, the process was slow going. In April 1980, he launched a military rescue mission known as Operation Eagle Claw to rescue the hostages from the embassy compound. The rescue attempt failed, however, due to a desert sandstorm that caused their helicopters to malfunction. This was a blow to the president. Americans thought he was unable to resolve the problem and was ineffective as a leader.

On January 21, 1981, just a few hours after President Ronald Reagan delivered his inaugural address, the students finally freed the hostages. Nonetheless, the hostage crisis had long-lasting effects on US–Iranian relations.

1980 PRESIDENTIAL ELECTION

In the 1980 election, President Jimmy Carter was seeking reelection on the Democratic ticket. Ronald Reagan was the Republican running against him. Many people say that due to the ongoing Iranian hostage crisis, Carter was not effective as a president. Reagan won the election in a landslide, receiving the highest number of electoral votes ever won by a nonincumbent candidate.

CHAPTER FIVE

1981 TO 2000

In the final decades of the 20th century, the
United States was well on its way to seeing a
change in foreign relations. President Ronald
Reagan's approach to communism and the
Cold War sent a message to the world that the
United States wanted to remain a global leader.

In these two decades, communism began to decrease as the former states of the Soviet Union transitioned to democracy.

Not only were there changes to foreign policy, a new domestic economic policy was introduced. "Reaganomics" brought some of the greatest economic growth the United States had ever seen. Advancements in technology set the stage for average Americans to change their lifestyle and how they worked with the invention of home computers.

But wars abroad continued, and growing terrorism threats at home and overseas began to change the way Americans thought and acted.

President Ronald Reagan in 1982

The Reagan Revolution: 1980–1989

Throughout the 1960s and 1970s, the United States economy experienced **inflation**. This meant that everyday goods—like food and clothing—became more expensive. At the same time, many people were out of work. When President Ronald Reagan entered office, he knew the United States needed a new economic plan. This plan became known as "Reaganomics," and it was built on four key goals: reduce government spending, lower taxes, lessen governmental regulations, and control inflation to keep prices in check.

At the core of this plan was a belief that a tax cut would put more money into people's wallets. Reagan thought it would encourage those with money to invest in businesses and the stock market in hopes of making more money. Reagan also expected that people would then spend their money on more goods, like clothing, cars, and houses. This would then help businesses, and the government, grow.

Reagan believed this growth would then "trickle down" to everyone. The trickle-down effect would work if those whose wealth increased spent a portion of the wealth back into the economy. New jobs could be created, wages would rise, and more tax revenues could help fund public programs such as education, healthcare, and welfare programs for the elderly and the poor.

To some extent, these policies

MEET RONALD REAGAN

Ronald Reagan was the 40th president of the United States and served two terms, from 1981 to 1989. His presidency was marked by a restoration of national prosperity through his economic plan. He is also known for encouraging friendly foreign relations and his role in helping the fall of communism. His contributions can still be felt today.

worked. Inflation came down and the prices of goods evened out. More people found jobs. The economy began to grow again. Today, however, economists debate whether these policies had the desired effect in the long term. Nonetheless, the ideas and policies of the 1980s continue to impact us today. Reagan's **conservatism** appealed to many people at the time because of the tax cuts and idea of a smaller government. When he left office in 1989, Ronald Reagan had the highest approval rating since the presidency of Franklin D. Roosevelt.

FREE MARKET ECONOMICS

A free market economy is a loosely regulated system of economic exchange. This means that a government's control over taxes, quotas, tariffs, and other forms of economic oversight exist, but are minimal. In other words, companies can make and sell their goods without much government interference or oversight. Many people wonder, however, if there is ever really a true free market economy, since some control always exists.

Sandra Day O'Connor in 1981

A First for the Supreme Court: 1981

On September 25, 1981, Sandra Day O'Connor made history by becoming the first woman to be unanimously approved to the nation's highest court, and she was sworn in as a United States Supreme Court Justice.

O'Connor was working as a judge for the Arizona Court of Appeals when President Ronald Reagan chose her in 1981 to fill the Supreme Court seat of a retiring justice. The appointment was part of a promise President Reagan made during his presidential campaign when he vowed to appoint a female judge

It took nearly 200 years before the first woman was appointed to the US Supreme Court. Since then, only four women have sat on the bench. President Ronald Reagan appointed the first one, Sandra Day O'Connor, in 1981. Justice O'Connor served until her retirement in January, 2006. In 1993, President Bill Clinton appointed Ruth Bader Ginsburg. And while President Barack Obama was in office, he appointed two women: Sonia Sotomayor in 2009, and Elena Kagan in 2010.

to the Supreme Court. O'Connor was chosen out of a candidacy pool of 12 other people.

As with most Supreme Court nominations, the selection of O'Connor was criticized. She was known as a moderate conservative and faced opposition from those who had different views on certain topics. She was ultimately unanimously endorsed, however, and was sworn in as the 102nd justice of the US Supreme Court.

As a Supreme Court Justice, O'Connor proved to be one who could think for herself. She was regarded as a practical conservative, but she often voted with the liberal justices on social issues. She was also known for her ability to moderate the other justices. She announced her plan to retire in 2005, and was replaced by Samuel Alito.

ALASKA DEPARTMENT OF ENVIRONMENTAL CONSERVATION V. EPA

One court case for which O'Connor ruled with the majority (like most of the other judges) was the case of *Alaska Department of Environmental Conservation v. EPA*. The Supreme Court ruled that the Environmental Protection Agency could step in and take action to reduce air pollution under the Clean Air Act (CAA) when a state conservation agency fails to act on it. Under the act, individual states have the authority to decide when a company is making its best efforts to control pollution. In this case, however, the EPA stepped in to say the state had to do more.

An Apple computer lab in 1979

The Personal Computer and the Internet: 1980s

Although computer technologies had been around for many years, it was not until the late 1970s and early 1980s that computers were made affordable and small enough for home use.

In 1958, Robert Noyce and Jack Kilby introduced the integrated circuit, or **microchip**, which helped computers process information quickly and made it possible for engineers to start thinking about building smaller machines. Ten years later, the tech company Intel was formed. In 1981, IBM introduced the first personal computer, the Model 5150,

Technology was something Bill Gates loved from an early age. He wrote his very first computer software program when he was only 13 years old. By the time he was in college, he and his friend Paul Allen worked together to develop software for the first microcomputers. Bill and Paul formed Microsoft, a company that became a worldwide technology trailblazer.

informally called Acorn. It ran on an operating system created by Microsoft, a company founded by Paul Allen and Bill Gates. Using a memory chip from Intel, floppy disks for storing information, and an optional color monitor, the machine marked a historic step forward in personal computing.

The next big advancement came when the internet was developed. Originally funded by the US Department of Defense in the late 1960s, the internet took a giant step forward in 1983 when researchers began developing a system of computer networks that joined together. The internet had a huge impact on people's daily lives—soon computer work could be accessed from home, researching a topic was as easy as clicking a button, information could be transmitted faster than ever before, and people could communicate through email and even purchase goods online.

SILICON VALLEY

Silicon Valley is the region in Northern California that represents the rise of the internet, the digital world, and tech wealth. Located just south of the San Francisco Bay, it is where many technology adventurists go when trying to set up a new business or gain inspiration because they hope their luck will follow the others who came before them.

Operation Desert Storm in 1991

The Persian Gulf War: 1990-1991

In 1990, tensions were growing in the Middle East between the countries of Iraq and Kuwait. Iraq's leader, Saddam Hussein, accused Kuwait of drilling above its quota of crude oil from the Ar-Rumaylah oil fields along the common border of the two nations. Hussein started moving troops to the border. President Hosni Mubarak of Egypt tried to negotiate peace between the two nations, but on August 2, 1990, Iraq invaded neighboring Kuwait. Kuwait then turned to the United States for help.

The United Nations formed a coalition of approximately 39 countries, led by the United States, to help Kuwait. In January 1991, the United States began an air offensive over Iraq's defenses, then its communications, weapons, and even oil refineries. They wanted to cut off Iraq's resources to make them stop the war. This coalition was known as Operation Desert Storm. In February, the coalition forces switched to ground attacks. This became known as Operation Desert Sabre. This 100-hour fight defeated the Iraqis and freed Kuwait.

On February 28, 1991, President George H. W. Bush declared a ceasefire, and the Persian Gulf War ended. In agreement with the peace treaty, Iraq

MEET GEORGE H. W. BUSH

George H. W. Bush was the 41st president of the United States. In his inaugural speech, he pledged to use American strength as "a force for good." One of the biggest tests of foreign policy under his term was when Saddam Hussein invaded Kuwait. President Bush, along with the United Nations, sent troops and defeated Iraq's million-man army. Although President Bush had a lot of success diplomatically, it was not enough to help him get reelected in 1992.

would have to recognize Kuwait as a free nation and get rid of all their weapons of mass destruction.

SMART BOMBS

The laser-guided bombs used during the Persian Gulf War were called "smart bombs" because they were very accurate in hitting their targets. These bombs greatly changed how the war was fought. Smart bombs helped destroy a large and well-equipped Iraqi army before the land battle even began.

Taking down the Berlin Wall in 1989

The End of the Cold War: 1991

When he moved into the Oval Office, President Ronald Reagan took a different stand against communism. He called the Soviet Union an "evil empire" and wanted the United States to bring peace and freedom to other parts of the world. To do this, Reagan said the United States would have to be the world's most powerful military presence, so he spent billions of dollars on new weapons. The Soviet Union tried to keep up, but it couldn't afford to spend heavily on weapons while continuing to feed its people.

Mikhail Gorbachev led the Communist Party beginning in 1985 and became the president of the

Mikhail Gorbachev became the first president of the Soviet Union in 1990, but he resigned in 1991. He promoted peaceful international relations. Gorbachev is credited for ending the Cold War and for the fall of the Berlin Wall. Gorbachev won the Nobel Peace Prize in 1990 for his role in ending the Cold War and his contributions toward making a better world.

Soviet Union in 1990. When he rose to power, he knew that big changes needed to happen in the country. Gorbachev and Reagan met several times in the mid-to-late 1980s, and in 1987, they signed an agreement to reduce their number of arms. This marked the beginning of the end of the Cold War. Gorbachev began pulling troops out of Eastern Europe, and he forged ahead with both economic and political reforms that would eventually lead to the collapse of the Soviet Union.

In 1989, Poland became the first country behind the **Iron Curtain** to hold a democratic election. Although the Soviets tried to censor what the citizens heard on the radio and read in the newspapers, people were protesting in the streets. Other communist governments began to fall one by one. Gorbachev encouraged the movement.

The ultimate tipping point to the end of the Cold War occurred in the city of Berlin, Germany. The Berlin Wall had divided the city for 28 years. As people saw communist governments falling, protestors were encouraged to force open the border. In November 1989, citizens on both sides of the Berlin Wall attacked it with axes and sledgehammers. The Berlin Wall fell, and Germany was on its way to becoming a unified country once again.

PERESTROIKA AND GLASNOST

In 1985, Gorbachev launched perestroika, or social and political restructuring, when he became the head of the Communist Party. He pushed reform toward a semi-mixed economy, edging out communism. Gorbachev next launched glasnost, or openness and sharing of information, because he believed that opening up the political system was the only way for it to work. It also allowed people in the political process and the media to have more freedom of expression.

A memorial for the Oklahoma City bombing in 2015

Unrest at Home and Abroad: 1990s

The 1990s were a time of strife both at home and overseas. The Oklahoma City bombing in 1995 was the deadliest terrorist attack on US soil up to that point. Timothy McVeigh and Terry Nichols, two **extremist** and anti-government militants, carried out the bombing, which killed 168 people. A year later, another terrorist detonated bombs at a park in Atlanta, Georgia, at a free rock concert during the Summer Olympics being held there.

After two decades of sending bombs through the mail, Ted Kaczynski, known as the Unabomber, was captured in 1996 at his remote cabin in Lincoln,

The Federal Bureau of Investigation, or FBI, has one main goal: uphold and enforce the criminal laws of the United States. Guarding against terrorist attacks is chief among its priorities. The FBI works closely with partners at home and abroad to isolate terroristic threats and cut off financial aid or other support to terrorists. Through the years, terrorism has changed, but the FBI has remained ready to protect citizens. There is a Joint Terrorism Task Force and a Terrorist Screening Center that also provide services to keep America safe from terrorists.

Montana. He sent the first mail bomb through the US Postal Service in 1978. During his time in hiding, he staged 14 attacks (with 16 bombs), killing three people and injuring 23 others. Kaczynski wrote an essay describing how modern technology was bad for society and sent it to newspapers in 1995, demanding that it be published. In exchange for publishing it, he said there would be no more bombs. It was published, but soon after, he was caught. He was sentenced to eight life sentences without parole.

In February 1997, a Palestinian gunman named Ali Hassan Abu Kamal opened fire on tourists at an observation deck atop the Empire State Building in New York City. He killed one person and wounded six others before turning the gun on himself. A handwritten note carried by the gunman claimed this was a punishment attack against the "enemies of Palestine."

This homegrown terrorism was disturbing on so many levels, and was not confined to the United States. Osama bin Laden, the leader of the terrorist group Al Qaeda, was planning a surprise attack on the United States that would shock the world on September 11, 2001. With advancements in technology, it became easier to join a radical group without anyone knowing about it. It also became easier for extremists to communicate and pass information to one another.

GUN CONTROL

Gun control is a highly controversial topic in the United States. Those against gun control point to the Second Amendment to the Constitution, which states that US citizens have the right to keep and bear arms. But others argue that having fewer guns will save lives.

LOOKING AHEAD

America during the 20th century was a time of much growth and change. When you look at the United States over this span of 100 years, you have to ask yourself: How did Americans achieve all these advancements?

Significant advancements came in technology, from the Wright brothers' first successful airplane flight to Neil Armstrong walking on the Moon. Americans also enjoyed advancements in the entertainment industry. Radios brought news into people's homes; later, televisions brought the screen to life; and then the personal computer and internet allowed individuals to have instant access to information. All these technologies helped pave the way for how we carry on with our lives today.

Social activists were also busy making many positive changes during the 20th century. Women gained

the right to vote with the passage of the 19th Amendment and later were promised equal treatment in the workplace with the Women's Liberation Movement. The civil rights movement opened doors for Black Americans to live as equals in society. Even the hippie counterculture movement introduced new foods and fads in music and fashion. These things happened because there was a desire for change, and people were courageous enough to take a stand and demand it.

All these achievements are why we can enjoy the things we do now. Every day, new technologies replace yesterday's version, and with each new advancement, we move forward. The same can be said for social change. As a nation, we must continue moving forward and growing for all future generations.

GLOSSARY

bootlegging: The illegal manufacture, distribution, or sale of goods, especially alcohol or musical recordings

communism: A political system in which business, property, and goods are owned by the government

conservatism: An approach that favors policies that support smaller government and traditional values, and does not like rapid changes

credit: The ability to obtain goods or services before paying, trusting the customer will pay later

extremist: A person who holds extreme or fanatical political views, especially someone who resorts to extreme violent action

fascism: An authoritarian political philosophy marked by strong national pride and a strong ruler with almost complete power

flapper: A fashionable young woman in the 1920s who rebelled against conventional standards of behavior

inflation: A rise in prices of goods and services

Iron Curtain: The political and military barrier put up by the Soviet Union after World War II to separate Eastern European allies from contact with the West and other noncommunist nations

isolationism: A policy of remaining separate or apart from the dealings of other groups or countries

mass production: The process of making large numbers of a product quickly

microchip: A tiny computer part that processes information quickly

propeller: A mechanical device with two or more angled blades that are used as a way to move a boat or aircraft

race riot: An outbreak of violence that is caused by prejudice, anger, or hatred against people of color

rationing: Limiting how much of certain goods people can buy

transatlantic flight: The flight of an aircraft across the Atlantic Ocean

RESOURCES

Books

Hubbard, Ben. *Space Race: The Story of Space Exploration to the Moon and Beyond.* Hauppauge, NY: B. E. S. Publishing, 2019.

Medina, Nico. *What Was the Berlin Wall?* New York: Penguin Workshop, 2019.

Pinkney, Andrea Davis, and Brian Pinkney. *Martin Rising: Requiem for a King.* New York: Scholastic Press, 2018.

Woolf, Alex. *Trailblazers: Neil Armstrong: First Man on the Moon.* New York: Random House Books for Young Readers, 2019.

Museums

Elvis Presley Museum at Graceland (Memphis, Tennessee)

The Museum of Flight (Seattle, Washington)

The National Center for Civil and Human Rights Museum (Atlanta, Georgia)

Websites

BaseballHall.org

NASA.gov

PBS.org

REFERENCES

Biography.com. "Charles Lindbergh." Last
modified February 5, 2020. biography.com
/historical-figure/charles-lindbergh.

———. "Walt Disney." Last modified August 21, 2019.
biography.com/business-figure/walt-disney.

Crouch, Tom D. "Samuel Pierpont Langley."
Encyclopaedia Britannica. Accessed
April 24, 2020. britannica.com/biography
/Samuel-Pierpont-Langley.

Encyclopaedia Britannica. "Spirit of St. Louis." Last
modified December 11, 2018. britannica.com
/topic/Spirit-of-Saint-Louis.

Franklin D. Roosevelt Presidential Library and
Museum. "Eleanor Roosevelt Biography."
Accessed April 24, 2020. fdrlibrary.org
/er-biography.

Friedel, Frank, and Hugh Sidey. "Herbert Hoover."
WhiteHouse.gov; reprinted from *The Presidents
of the United States of America*. Accessed April 22,
2020. whitehouse.gov/about-the-white-house
/presidents/herbert-hoover.

———. "Ronald Reagan." WhiteHouse.gov; reprinted from *The Presidents of the United States of America*. Accessed April 14, 2020. whitehouse.gov/about-the-white-house/presidents/ronald-reagan/.

———. "Woodrow Wilson." WhiteHouse.gov; reprinted from *The Presidents of the United States of America*. Accessed April 16, 2020. whitehouse.gov/about-the-white-house/presidents/woodrow-wilson/.

History.com. "The Great Migration." Last modified January 16, 2020. history.com/topics/black-history/great-migration.

———. "Iran Hostage Crisis." Last modified October 24, 2019. history.com/topics/middle-east/iran-hostage-crisis.

———. "New Deal." Last modified November 27, 2019. history.com/topics/great-depression/new-deal.

———. "Oklahoma City Bombing." Last modified May 20, 2020. history.com/topics/1990s/oklahoma-city-bombing.

———. "Panama Canal." Last modified September 30, 2019. Accessed April 14, 2020. history.com/topics/landmarks/panama-canal.

Joseph, Paul. *The Wright Brothers*. Minneapolis, MN: Abdo & Daughters, 1997.

Pfeiffer, Lee. "The Jazz Singer." Last modified April 11, 2019. britannica.com/topic/The-Jazz-Singer -film-1927.

———. "William Crawford Gorgas." Encyclopaedia Britannica. Last modified September 29, 2019. britannica.com/biography/William -Crawford-Gorgas.

Poets.org. "Langston Hughes." Accessed April 24, 2020. poets.org/poet/langston-hughes.

Sparks, Evan. "Raymond Orteig." Philanthropy Roundtable. Accessed April 15, 2020. philanthropyroundtable.org/almanac/people /hall-of-fame/detail/raymond-orteig.

Suddath, Claire. "A Brief History of Mickey Mouse." *Time*, November 18, 2008. content.time.com /time/arts/article/0,8599,1859935,00.html.

Wilkerson, Isabel. "The Long-Lasting Legacy of the Great Migration." *Smithsonian Magazine*, September 2016. Accessed April 15, 2020. smithsonianmag.com/history/long-lasting -legacy-great-migration-180960118.

ACKNOWLEDGMENTS

Thank you to Barbara Isenberg, my editor, for all your feedback and suggestions throughout the process. You were a tremendous help. Thank you to my family for your love, support, and understanding. I could not have written this book without your support first.

ABOUT THE AUTHOR

Andrea Bentley is an educator and the curriculum designer of Right Down the Middle with Andrea. She is a wife and mother who enjoys creating, reading, Sunday dinners, and making memories with her family.

CPSIA information can be obtained
at www.ICGtesting.com
Printed in the USA
JSHW010806210921
18853JS00001B/2